Supercharge Your Startup!

Creating a Powerful Vision and Business Plan in 5 Easy Steps

K.C. Hildreth

ISBN:
ISBN-13: 978-1496144881
ISBN 10: 1496144880

DEDICATION

To Neha. Your love and support makes everything possible.

ACKNOWLEDGEMENTS

Special thanks to my clients, friends and family. I am very grateful for your unswerving encouragement and support.

OTHER BOOKS BY K.C. HILDRETH

Living Into Your Highest Potential
3 Key Steps to Personal Growth

Fund Your Dreams!
Proven Tools for Pitching Investors

CONTENTS

PREFACE

This book is one of a series of books on Success, Entrepreneurship, Organizational Culture, and, in the future, many other topics related to human creativity, performance and growth. All of my books are intended as an introduction to topics that can be, and I believe should be, explored in more detail. For ease of access they are purposefully short and easy to digest. I encourage you to test, explore and learn more about each topic so that you can expand upon what I have written. In my work with clients I stress that the process of learning and growing is highly unique to each person and occurs best when *you decide you want to expand*. If you want the knowledge in this book to trigger something, then it will. I can only offer you the processes and information that I know to be effective. I hope it works for you!

If you need help, I am available.

K.C. Hildreth

www.kchildreth.com

INTRODUCTION

This book is written for those hardy souls who are either thinking about starting a business, have an existing business they would like to grow, or who would simply like to provide more structure and purpose to their existing enterprise. The tools that follow seek to simplify the process of business planning so that you can get the most out of your precious time. If you have already started your company you know that you do not have the luxury of hundreds of hours and the dedicated team necessary to create a complete strategic plan. Nor do you need to.

I know first hand that starting a company is challenging. I have founded or co-founded 8 companies over the past 40 years, and with each one I have learned more than I ever expected. One of the most powerful lessons I have taken away is the importance of a good vision and plan...but not for the reasons you might think. In fact, the whole notion of a 'plan' has morphed significantly since I graduated from business school many years ago.

Many people (including myself in the past) mistakenly believe that a business plan needs to be 50 pages of detailed analysis and research in order to be effective. This is simply not true. The purpose of a business plan is first and foremost to *direct your thinking and energy*, not to think of everything that could happen in the future. To call it a 'plan' is, actually, somewhat deceiving. In reality, a business plan is more of an 'educated hypothesis' than anything else. When you plan your business you are saying, in essence, 'here is what I am going to create, and how I think it will happen.' You can no more to predict or control the outcome than you can read the future. In fact, the plan loses it relevance the moment it is completed because the *actual* begins to replace the *hypothetical*.

As strange as it sounds, you really don't even need to use your plan for it to be effective. In my 30 years of entrepreneurial and business experience I have never *looked* at a business plan once it was completed. Indeed, even professional investors will usually only read the executive summary and spreadsheets in order to get the gist of the business and your assumptions. Most of their decision will be based on their confidence in you and the clarity of your intentions. The plan itself is just a stack of paper that says 'I did my homework'. By itself, it has no real importance.

So why create a plan in the first place? If nobody reads it, and you won't use it going forward, then why take the time to write one? I thought the same thing myself until I realized that the value lies in the *process* more than the *product*. Every time I have worked on a plan I have been forced to do research, think, write, edit, revisit, and think again. With each draft I noticed how I gained more confidence, sharpened my intentions, and became more and more of an expert in my subject. The process was not to help others understand what I was doing…but to help *me* to clarify what I was trying to create.

To reiterate: When you write a plan you are pointing your creative energy in a particular direction. You are teaching yourself to become directed and purposeful. You are putting a 'point' on the arrow of your mind. Every bit of thought, research and writing you do brings power and specificity to your endeavor and, as a result, convinces your prospective investors, customers and employees that you know what you are doing.

A simple, short and well thought out plan allows you to tell your story with clarity and passion. When you think through your idea from top to bottom and convey it in a short document you show mastery of the concepts. This process gives you the confidence to convey the idea, get excited about the future and answer any doubts about the outcome. A massive plan that 'boils the ocean' simply cannot do this because the very act of writing the plan becomes a project by itself. In my experience huge plans are overwhelming and 'under-interesting'.

In this guide I will show you how to create a plan that, while it seems to come from very simple beginnings, will both direct your energy and inspire your audiences. Your plan will be purposefully simple and short. You will have to do research, but only to the extent that it supports your main message. If you are, at some point in the future, going to seek millions of dollars in financing, then there is another level to the plan that may indeed take 50 pages. But for now all we are going to do is look at the core of your idea in order to give you confidence and focus.

My process contains five main steps, and each step leads to the next. At a high level the steps are as follows:

1. The word: (One word that represents your idea/business)
2. The sentence: (One line that expands on the word)
3. The paragraph: (3-6 sentences that give detail to the sentence)
4. The summary: (2 pages that explain the ideas in the paragraph)
5. The numbers: (A spreadsheet that justifies the financial conclusions in the summary)

These steps clearly support each other in a top down fashion. I like to call this 'pyramid thinking' because it can be represented visually as follows:

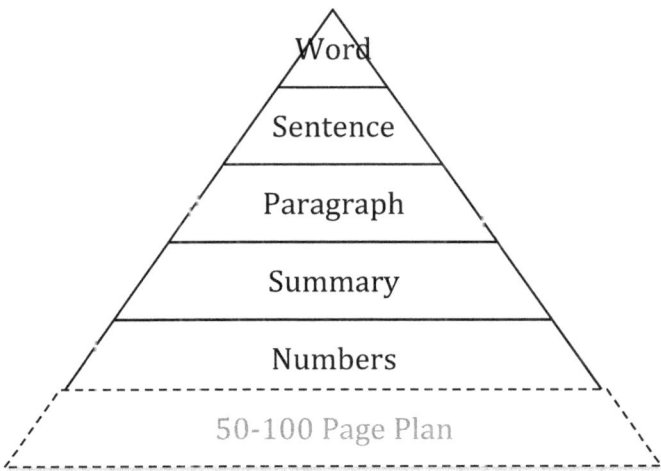

The base of the pyramid is wider because it contains more information. The "Word" is the central thought behind the "Sentence", and the "Paragraph" gives the sentence even more detail. At each step you will provide more information and 'color'. If you wanted you could theoretically take this down to the tiny details that virtually nobody else would find interesting (like number of pencils you will need, etc.). There may be a time in the future when you will want to take your work to a greater level of detail (ie. 50-100 pages), which you can create from the summary and numbers you produce in these exercises. However, in this book, are we going to work on creating a plan that guides, inspires and describes.

This book is organized to first teach you the concepts and then give you exercises and examples. Steps 1-5 explain each part of the process, while Appendices A-E give you exercises and examples. I recommend that you first read through everything, and then go back to Step 1, re-read the section and try the exercise in Appendix A. Once you have completed Step 1, then go to Step 2 and repeat. Keep in mind, however, that you may jump around and iterate between sections. This is OK and natural. Rarely does everything happen in a linear fashion, so if you find yourself struggling with one step feel free to jump to another and then return later. *The goal is to learn and clarify your thinking.*

So let's get started…and remember to have fun! Starting or planning a business is an exciting and inspiring process!

STEP 1: THE WORD

Although this might seem a silly step at first, it is actually the most important part of the process. This is because 'the word' is the beginning of your creation. Indeed, virtually every major religion ascribes divinity to 'the word' because words are the way that we transfer our thoughts into reality. Words represent thought, and thoughts create reality. We must therefore choose our words with care. Every single sound we utter casts an energetic wave into the world around us. As we speak we create. It all starts with the first word!

Another reason we are starting with one word is because it is very tempting for an excited entrepreneur to babble on and on about what s/he is trying to do. I have attended many investor 'pitch meetings' where the founder of a company is trying desperately to convey something powerful but cannot seem to say it simply. The result is a lot of head-scratching as people try to figure out the 'gist' of the business idea.

In order to create clarity around your idea and provide a foundation for the rest of the plan, you need to boil all your thoughts into *one word* about your business. That word should do two things:

1. Describe the central meaning of your business
2. Resonate (feel good) with the listener

Now you might think that number 1 is the most important, but it is NOT. The descriptiveness of the word is helpful but not nearly as meaningful as the power that the word conveys. The word you choose must have a deeper meaning to both you and the listener, but especially to you. This is because this word represents the *energy and meaning behind your idea.* If the word you choose is neutral then your whole idea will come across as neutral and flat. If the word is meaningful then it will resonate and create excitement in whoever reads or hears it.

Examples of 'flat' vs. 'resonant' words"

- Style (flat) vs. Beauty (meaningful and resonant)
- Architecture (flat) vs. Home (meaningful and resonant)
- Excellence (flat) vs. Love (meaningful and resonant)
- Medical (flat) vs. Care (meaningful and resonant)

The words on the left certainly have meaning, but they do not have any emotion. 'Flat' words merely describe *what* you are doing, whereas the more resonant words give the reader a feeling about *why* you are doing it as well. Ultimately, the most resonant and meaningful word you can use is 'Love' because anything created from

Love and with Love is incredibly powerful. Many religions and philosophies contend that Love is the original creative feeling and therefore the foundation of all that is. When something is done from Love it instantly connects, attracts and creates.

When you choose your word, try to find the feeling of love in it as you say it to yourself. Think of the higher purpose and deeper meaning behind what you are doing. If you can't find a deeper meaning, then you may need to shift the nature of what you are trying to accomplish. "Making Money" is not deep or meaningful and will not resonate with your customers, employees or potential investors. Most lasting, powerful businesses were built to help, guide, be of service, or some other meaningful purpose. As you find *your* purpose, you will also find your inspiration and willingness to do what it takes to be successful.

Some examples of emotive, meaningful words are: Care, Connection, Grace, Wholeness, Home, Beauty, Friendship, Joy, Health, Healing, Peace, Kindness, Compassion, Purpose, Possibility and Affection. Your word will have meaning to you, and it will convey that meaning to others as you speak it. The key is to *feel* your word, not think it.

When you are ready, go to Appendix A and play with some potential words that might describe your business.

STEP 2: THE SENTENCE

Once you have chosen your word, you can now create a sentence that expands on the word. This sentence is important because it will become the foundation of your entire plan and will be the short answer when someone asks you 'what are you working on?' In my experience it is very rare for an entrepreneur (or any person for that matter) to concisely present what they are doing in one sentence! This is why it is so important! The ability to express something powerful in one sentence shows that the speaker is someone thoughtful and prepared

If you are pitching your business or product to an investor or customer and you cannot describe it in one concise statement, it shows a lack of attention to what you are offering. A listener must be able to grasp the entirety of your idea with little confusion and few questions. This is especially true in terms of the 'why' behind what you are doing, because this is where the power lies. If you have a powerful 'why' and a good description of 'what' then virtually any person should walk away nodding their head in understanding.

I like to think the ultimate test is with a stranger on the street... 'average Joe'. If, upon hearing your sentence, Joe would immediately 'get' what you are working on, then you have hit the mark. If he can see a deeper 'why' in what you have said, then even better. If, however, he gives you that 'I don't get it' look, then you know you need to re-craft what you have written.

An example of a poorly written sentence is:

We are creating a best-in-class software solution to the problem of logistics management.

Huh? This is business-speak that has absolutely no resonance or meaning. A small subset of people in the logistics industry might understand what you are saying, but there is certainly no power behind it.

Re-done:

We develop truck-tracking software that makes the jobs of shipping industry employees easier and more joyful.

This sentence might seem overly simple but that is the point. When we are pitching an idea, we can never assume that people know what we are talking about, so we must keep our description clear and concise. Further, we want to let people know that we are doing this because we want to make people happy, which is the 'why' behind our 'what'. If we make people happy then we will definitely sell products. If we say we are 'best-in-class' then we will simply make people yawn.

Some key pitfalls to avoid in your sentence:

- Jargon. It is boring and limits your audience.
- Talking about money. If you are creating a business simply to make money, then you are building on a false foundation. Money is an *outcome*, not a purpose.
- Running on. Your sentence should be able to be said in one breath with no commas or pauses.

Some things to make sure you include:

- Your 'Word'. The sentence should be built around your word, and convey the meaning behind it (in the above example it would be 'joy').
- A description of what you intend to do   Surprisingly many people describe the concept and not what they actually are going to do. The listener should hear this right away. (in this case '...*develop track-tracking software*')
- The 'why' should be obvious (in this case '...*makes the jobs of shipping industry employees easier and more joyful*')

Very rarely will you hit the perfect sentence right away, so be patient. You may have to test it on multiple people before you get it just right.

Go to Appendix B and try out a sentence for yourself. Make sure to use the Word you chose in Appendix A.

STEP 3: THE PARAGRAPH

As you might have guessed, the next step is to expand your sentence into a paragraph. To make this process easier, I recommend that the sentence created in Step 2 become the first sentence of the paragraph. If written well the first line will flow naturally into the following sentences.

Your paragraph will have three purposes:

1. To give a more detailed overview of your idea
2. To act as a prompt for additional questions
3. To inspire the listener

As you write you will answer key questions about your business that the one sentence was unable to convey. Once finished the paragraph should provide you with a quick 'elevator pitch' that gives the listener a fairly complete overview of your intentions but not enough such that they won't have any other questions. Your paragraph should sound interesting and provocative!

The structure of the paragraph will generally take the following form (although it may vary depending on your business). Each number represents an idea, but might not be a separate sentence. See if you can combine these ideas so that you end up with 3-6 sentences. Your ability to craft thoughts into as few words as possible is what will make your intentions clear and powerful:

> 1. Your sentence from above. 2. WHY this is a great opportunity right now. 3. HOW you intend to do what you say in the first sentence. 4. WHERE you intend to do this. 5. WHEN you intend to execute on your plan. 6. WHO you intend to work with. 7. WHAT you need to execute. 8. WHY you are doing this.

This format creates a 'full circle' starting with a powerful first sentence and ending with a statement of purpose, or 'why'. Within the paragraph virtually all the major questions are answered. Just like the sentence from Step 2, the goal is to have the listener nod their head in understanding when they hear your idea. They may have additional questions - which is good - but they will at least get the gist of your idea and plan.

Your language and tone is important because you want the listener to be excited by your idea, especially if you are speaking about it. The words you use should be resonant, positive and attractive. As you write you want to feel the energy flowing out of you! Allow yourself to get excited! People are inspired by *people who are inspired*. Inspire yourself! Don't be afraid to use colorful and uplifting language, because it will definitely have an impact. The last thing you want to do is leave the reader/listener flat.

Be patient with this process. Your paragraph may take multiple edits and versions. You may see things in your sentence and word that you would like to change, and this is natural. Remember, this entire process is first and foremost meant to *clarify and focus your thinking*. As you work with your thoughts and words you will be forced to ask yourself hard questions This is the point of the entire process.

So just give it a try and see what comes up! Appendix C will guide you through the process and give you an example. You can't fail, you can only learn!

STEP 4: THE SUMMARY

You are probably getting the idea at this point, but I will reiterate what we are doing anyway! The Summary is a two-page (approximately) document that gives more detail to the paragraph you constructed above. This summary will give any reader enough information to thoroughly understand your business. Typically an investor or other observer will need only this document to decide whether or not they are interested in your project. More importantly, after you write these two pages you will have been prompted to think through all the major questions that confront any business owner.

There are ten areas you will be addressing in this summary, and each has a number of questions you will want to answer. Your level of description will be highly dependent on your business, but the general questions are the same for most companies. In order, they are:

1. **The idea** (This usually either includes or is a copy of the paragraph you wrote above in step 3.)

    a.   What is the idea?

    b.   What is the mission and vision of the company (in short)?

    c.   Why is it compelling?

2. **The market** (The number of people who will buy what you are selling. If you are a local business it could be a subset of your city…if you are national, it could be a percentage of the country or world. You may have to do some research to get an idea of how many potential customers there are, but this information is worth getting!)

    a.   How big is the market? How many people?

    b.   Who buys the product (age, gender, demographics)?

    c.   Why do they buy it?

3. **The product** (The things or service you are offering for sale. You want to give a good description, perhaps including pictures.)

    a.   What are you offering, and in what variations?

    b.   Why is it interesting?

4. **Operations** (How you intend to make or fulfill your product or service. This may take place in a manufacturing plant, office, or retail outlet, but there is always some sort of process to selling things. You will be describing that here.)

    a.   How do you intend to make the product?

    b.   What machines are you going to need?

    c.   Where will you get your raw material?

    d.   How are you going to keep and manage inventory?

    e.   How do you intend to service your product (returns, etc)?

5. **Technology** (This section is mainly to describe your web site and what it will be able to do. Describe in simple terms what your web presence will look like.)

    a.   What capabilities will your web site have?

    b.   Will people be able to buy from it?

6. **Marketing and Sales** (Every product needs to be sold through a 'channel', which is simply the way it gets to the customer. In this section you will tell the reader how you will get people interested in your product and how they will be able to buy it.)

    a.   How do you intend on selling your product (ie internet or other)?

    b.   Will you sell direct or through retail channels?

    c.   How do you intend on marketing your company and product (ie internet, advertising, other)?

    d.   If a consumer product, how will it be branded?

    e.   Are there any special strategies to sell lots of product?

7. **Business Model** (This is a verbal description of how you will make money selling your product and where that money will come from. **This section ties closely with Step 5: The Numbers**. The story you tell in this section should match closely with the story you are telling with the spreadsheet.)

    a. How do you intend to price the product (ie low cost provider, or high end, or both)?

    b. Where will most of your revenues come from?

    c. Where will most of your costs come from?

    d. What will be your profit margin?

    e. Why are you going to make a lot of money?

8. **Strategy and Competitive Landscape** (An overview of all the companies in your industry and where you fit, especially if they are in direct competition with you. If you are a local business, then it will be similar local businesses in the area. If not, then it might be all the businesses in the world that do what you do. Either way, you will want to differentiate yourself and sell your uniqueness.)

    a. Who else is doing this?

    b. What are they doing?

    c. How much business do they do?

    d. Why are you different or special?

    e. Why is there room for you too?

9. **Financing needs and Corporate Structure** (Every company needs to have a 'corporate structure' which simply describes how it is formed and who owns it. If you have a formal "company" with an Inc. at the end, it will have shareholders. If you have a partnership then you will have partners. Sole proprietors (which simply means one person *is* the company) don't have a formal legal structure except for maybe a DBA ("doing business as"), yet they are valid forms of business. When a company is founded it also needs cash to get off the ground. How much will you need and why? Outline your intentions in this section. You will likely need to educate yourself around these subjects, so don't get intimidated. Just do what you can and learn.)

     a. How is the company organized (ie partnership, corporation, sole proprietorship? Is it wholly owned by you?)

     b. Where are you going to get your initial capital?

     c. How much more money are you going to need?

     d. How will you manage cash flow?

     e. Are you looking for outside investors?

10. **Bios** (The most important part of any business is its people, especially the founders. You will want to sell any reader why YOU – and/or your partners – are the right people for the job)

     a. Who is involved?

b.   What are their backgrounds?

c.   Why are they perfect for the job?

Given what I have outlined here, clearly it will be a struggle to keep it under 2 pages! And yet this is what I want you to do. When you are forced to be brief, you must go back and look for any information that is unnecessary. In my experience businesspeople put a LOT of unnecessary information in business plans. Every sentence should count, every word matter. As you edit, iterate and minimize, you will become very good at articulating what you are doing. This is a very important skill.

Remember that your ability to articulate your vision and plan is the driving energy behind your creative efforts. Overuse of words indicates a lack of focus. As you hone your message you also create a sharper, more effective business tool. Also, if you are seeking investment you must be extremely well versed in your arguments before you start speaking. Investors are not known to tolerate confused, blathering pitches. This step will help you keep your mind sharp.

As you are writing, you will likely want to include statistics that you currently don't have, or reference information that you have not yet learned. This is absolutely normal. In this case, simply put a 'blank' to remind yourself to get more information. For example, if you want to say that the market for your product is very large you can simply say:

'In the US alone there are over _____ consumers who
bought a similar product last year, and it is estimated that the
market will grow to _____ in 2015'.

After you are done with the draft, you can then go do some research
and 'fill in the blanks'. The key is not to allow yourself to be slowed
by what you don't know. Take your time and simply write what you
know. As you write you may find that you don't know as much as
you thought. This is fantastic because it will point you toward your
educational opportunities! Again, the point of this process is to
LEARN…so be patient and open your mind!

Appendix D contains a worksheet and an example that will help
you write your summary. When you are ready, go to that section and
get started.

K.C. HILDRETH

STEP 5: THE NUMBERS

The final, but very important, step in creating a concise plan is to generate financials that you can use to estimate future profits, budget for your expenditures and measure your sales. This is perhaps the most active part of your plan because in the next planning cycle, you will return to your original estimates to see how you have fared. Any differences will become the basis for an annual re-write of your plan.

This section, also called the financial plan, supports your 'Business Model' paragraph in the written summary. The numbers you show in your spreadsheet should represent the story you tell in your summary about how you are going to make money. If you say you are going to expand in the 6th month of your business, for example, then your spreadsheet should reflect the added costs in that month, and your write up should explicitly state your strategy behind expansion in that month. These two documents must tie together tightly.

There are two basic parts of a financial plan:

1. Your assumptions
2. The estimates in the spreadsheet itself

Before explaining these, it is important that you learn to use Excel or some other spreadsheet program. Spreadsheets are indispensible to any business and will become central to your planning and budgeting.

The first part of a plan, the assumptions, are what you will take as given for the entire document. Examples of assumptions include:

- The price of your product
- Initial unit sales
- Growth rates (i.e. month to month increases in sales or costs)
- Employee 'burden' (the cost of health care, etc, of each employee - usually a percentage of salary)

Once you have outlined your assumptions, you can then begin to put numbers into your spreadsheet. Below are blank examples of two parts of a spreadsheet*. As you can see, there is one sheet that represents the first year of your operations, and another that shows the later years. The first year is broken down into months because you want to be as specific as possible about your income estimates and costs. As you project into the future you will have less information and can therefore make it less specific.

*If you cannot read these spreadsheets or would like a free template, please go to kchildreth.com/freedownloads

							YEAR 1						
	Jan	Feb	Mar	Apr	May	Jun	Jul	Aug	Sep	Oct	Nov	Dec	Total
Revenues													
Revenue Stream 1													
Revenue Stream 2													
Revenue Stream 3													
Total Revenue													
Cost of Revenues													
Cost 1													
Cost 2													
Cost 3													
Net Direct Costs													
Net Revenues													
Costs													
Employees													
Employee 1													
Employee 2													
Employee 3													
Employee 4													
Rent													
Utilities													
Supplies Equip													
Legal Fees													
Accounting/Tax													
Professional Fees													
Marketing													
Travel													
Operating Expenses													
Web Development													
Site Management													
Net Costs													
Profit/Loss													

	YEAR 2								
	Q1	Q2	Q3	Q4	Total		Year 3	Year 4	Year 5
Revenues									
Revenue Stream 1									
Revenue Stream 2									
Revenue Stream 3									
Total Revenue									
Cost of Revenues									
Cost 1									
Cost 2									
Cost 3									
Net Direct Costs									
Net Revenues									
Costs									
Employees									
Employee 1									
Employee 2									
Employee 3									
Employee 4									
Rent									
Utilities									
Supplies Equip									
Legal Fees									
Accounting/Tax									
Professional Fees									
Marketing									
Travel									
Operating Expenses									
Web Development									
Site Management									
Net Costs									
Profit/Loss									

In Year 1 you will estimate monthly revenues and costs, Year 2 quarterly, and in Years 3-5 you will combine everything into one annual number. Don't worry if you have no idea how you will grow in years 3-5. Nobody does! You will simply use an assumed growth rate to estimate how fast your revenues and costs will increase from year to year. The ideal is to have your revenues increase much faster than your costs, as this is how you generate a profit!

To start, let's take a look at the line items on the left side of the spreadsheet. These are the revenue and cost estimates that you will use to generate your numbers. Your business may have different costs, so make sure to be thorough in your thought process.

1. **Revenue:** This is the money you will be bringing in from your operations. Usually it is the result of the simple calculation (price x volume). Figure out how many units you think you are going to sell each month then multiply it by the average price per unit. If you have many offerings, you might want to have a line item for each type of revenue. If you have only a few, then you can calculate an average price and then multiply by units. Either way, play around with the numbers until you think you have an accurate representation of revenues per month for the first few months. Then you can assume a 'growth rate', which is the amount that revenues increase month over month. As you operate the company this number will become more predictable because you will have actual data with which to compare these estimates.

2. **Cost of Revenues:** The accounting term for this is 'Cost of Goods Sold' or 'COGS'. It represents the direct costs of selling your product. A 'direct cost' is one that you can tie directly to the product, such as the wholesale price of the product itself. If you buy, say, a toaster for $11 and sell it for $20, then the 'Cost of Revenue' of that toaster is $11. You will subtract this from the revenues because it is not really your money in the first place...you only made $9 on the sale of the toaster.

3. **Net Revenues:** This is the total Revenue minus the total Cost of Revenues. This number is the real income from sales

and will be the basis from which you will subtract your ongoing costs.

4. **Employee Costs:** Typically the most significant operating cost is Employees. Every time you plan hire an employee you will add their salary to the month in which you plan to bring them on board. Each salary typically has a 'burden', which is the cost above salary of all employees. A burden can be health care, computer equipment, day care, or other benefits. Typically in planning we add a 50% burden to be conservative, although this number will more likely be around 25%.

5. **Rent:** A fairly straightforward calculation, but make sure to account for expansion if you are predicting significantly increased sales volume over time.

6. **Utilities:** Gas, electric, etc.

7. **Equipment:** This is both the initial purchase of equipment (which will be a large lump-sum in the first months, unless financed), and then the budget allocated for equipment purchases over the months. Depending on your business this can be large or small.

8. **Legal Fees:** A budgeted amount for your lawyers.

9. **Accounting/Tax:** Same as legal fees.

10. **Marketing:** To estimate marketing costs you must first come up with a marketing plan and then allocate a monthly amount to pay for the plan.

11. **Travel:** If there is planned travel (for sales, etc) then estimate here.

12. **Web Development:** There will be up-front costs to develop your web site and then periodic costs to improve and overhaul it. Get an estimate from a developer and place the costs in this row.

13. **Site Management:** Your web site will have to be hosted and managed over time, and the cost will be dependent on its complexity and size. Your developer can help you with this.

The formula for this spreadsheet is very simple, and has been the underlying commerce calculation for thousands of years of 'business history':

	Total Revenue
(-)	Cost of Revenues
(=)	Net Revenue
(-)	Net Costs
(=)	**Profit (Loss)**

The money you make from selling your product, less what it costs to make or sell that product, equals your 'Net Revenue'. This is called the 'real' revenue number because you cannot call something revenue if it is really just the recouping of a cost. If, for example, I buy a chair for $50 and sell it to you for $100, I cannot say my 'real' revenue is $100 because half of that goes right out the door to pay for the chair! So my 'real' or 'Net' revenue number is $50.

Now, once you have the Net Revenue you can subtract the costs of running the business. These 'Net Costs' are the sum of all the expenses you incur while operating your enterprise. In the beginning your Net Costs are going to be higher than your Net Revenue, because you must get up and running and buy materials in order to sell anything in the first place. This is why the term 'Capitalism' was coined. When a business starts, it needs 'capital', or money, to get going because it will likely operate at a loss in the beginning.

So you take your Net Revenue and subtract your Net Costs, getting to the Profit or Loss for each period. Normally the first 3-6 months operate at a loss (sometimes longer for certain industries), and then as the company sells product the loss turns into a profit. You know how much 'capital' or start-up money you need by adding the total profits and losses over the first year and noting the final number. For example, assume your business generates the following profit(loss) over the first year:

> Jan   ($5,000)
> Feb   ($10,000)
> Mar   ($12,000)
> April ($15,000)
> May   ($8,000)
> June   ($4,000)
> July   ($500)
> Aug $1,000
> Sept $2,000
> Oct $4,000
> Nov $6,000
> Dec $8,000
> Total ($33,500)

This tells you that you need approximately $34,000 in start up capital to get your business up and running. To be conservative, I like to add a 50% buffer to these numbers in order to make sure I have enough to account for variability in my plan. So the final number would be $33,500 x 1.5, or $50,250. This should be enough to get you started, *if you have planned well.*

This is why thinking through your plan is so important. It is very risky to start a business with too little capital. If you underestimate your costs, you will run out of money. If you overestimate your revenues, you will also run out of money. The number 1 reason small companies fail is because they don't estimate their cash needs accurately. Investors and banks do not like to give money to companies that are strapped because the risks are too high. You must ensure that you really know your market and your costs. This knowledge will give you the confidence to ask for what you need or, if you are using your own money, help you feel secure in your investment.

After you finish the first year you can proceed to years 2-5. The second year you will be estimating quarterly, so all you need to do is attach a growth rate to the last three months of year 1. For example, if in October, November and December of year 1 you estimated combined revenues would be $10,000, you might add a growth rate of 10% to show that in the first quarter of year 2 your revenues would be $11,000 ($10,000 x 1.1). Each revenue and cost line would have an assumed growth rate across Q1, Q2, Q3 and Q4. Then you would do the same for year 3, year 4 and year 5. Once you have filled in all the numbers you should see a 'growth curve' across the profit(loss) line. In the beginning there will likely be a loss, and at the end of year 5 you will likely see a fairly large profit. The steepness of this growth curve is the potential of your business.

Stepping back, I want to reassure you that this is not as difficult as it is *detailed*. The concepts are not rocket science. People have been estimating these numbers since the first money was coined. The important part is, like the entire planning process, the thought you put into the estimates. You will need to think long and hard about how much you can sell, how much your goods will cost, and how much it will cost to run the company. This is a critical skill that, if you are seeking outside funds, an investor will need to see. *If you learn this skill you will increase the likelihood that you will be successful and gain the confidence of those who would support you.*

I recommend that you just start with what you know. Lay out your assumptions around unit sales, price, costs and employees. Then build a spreadsheet and put the more obvious numbers in the cells. Play around with what you don't know. Take guesses, do research. Ask people in the industry. Get to know your market. The key is to make estimates and then test those estimates as best you can. As you iterate the spreadsheet you will learn, and as you learn you will gain confidence. Eventually you will become an expert in your industry, and this is when you can start asking for money or feel good about investing your own.

Appendix E can help you get started on your spreadsheet. When you feel you are ready, take the step!

K.C. HILDRETH

CONCLUSION

Congratulations! You have just been through the basic steps of writing a business plan! As you can see, it is not terribly difficult if you take it step by step. Certainly there will be times when you are not sure of a particular detail, but that is OK because this process is intended to do exactly that: highlight the things you don't know. Once you know what you don't know, you can then 'fill in the blanks' and complete your learning.

Anyone who has ever been an entrepreneur or investor knows that you can't know everything. If I run across a business owner who claims to have all the answers…well then I know I have a problem. You can't ever know all things, but you can do your homework and at least identify the things you don't know. When you see the 'blank spots' in your knowledge, you can then come up with potential answers and at least be aware of the options. I am always very impressed by people who admit that they don't know something but have thought about what they might do in various situations. This shows openness, a willingness to learn, and flexibility in the face of uncertainty. These are precisely the attributes of a successful entrepreneur.

Once you have your two-page plan, you may decide to take it further and create a larger plan. This step merely requires taking each paragraph of your summary and giving it a chapter of its own. Your summary becomes an outline for a document with 7-10 chapters, plus supporting Appendices. This type of document is very impressive because of its structure. From 'The Word' on down it will appear cohesive and compelling.

In my experience the only reason for creating a larger plan is to seek investors for an already growing business. When you approach a large investor (i.e. an institution or venture capitalist), they will ask much more detailed questions about your assumptions and projections. You will need to take the plan to 'another level' and drill even deeper into your numbers and thought processes. This will require a plan that is most likely in the 50-75 page range and includes supporting research and documents. I have personally created plans that ran into the hundreds of pages including exhibits. The goal, however, is still the same: To learn about your industry and think through all the potential scenarios.

For most entrepreneurs, however, I encourage you to stick with the two-page plan until you are up and running. There is no reason to build a big plan to start or grow a company. After your first year I recommend that you revisit your original plan. Were you correct in your predictions? Did your strategy work? Were your numbers accurate? It is more than likely your answer to one of these questions will be 'no'. This is to be expected. As German military strategist Helmuth Von Moltke once said, "No battle plan survives contact with the enemy." The reality of a situation is always more complex and nuanced than can be understood by your structured mind. For that reason you must always treat a plan as a detailed hypothesis that organizes your thinking, nothing more.

Once completed, you will find that this effort is well worth the time. If you take the process seriously, your plan can keep you focused and directed toward your vision. From the moment you choose your 'word' you will find an energy and purpose that keeps you going when events get confusing. If you can re-envision your business and re-write this plan each year you are virtually guaranteed to be successful! Believe in yourself and never stop learning!

APPENDIX A: YOUR WORD

Take a moment to yourself and *feel* your word. What word represents *why* you are doing what you are doing? Does it feel good to you? Does it have meaning for you? Is it positive and uplifting? Would you be proud to speak your word to others? Would it inspire them? If so, write it below:

My word is: _____

    I choose this word because:

You may find that you need to experiment with words. I encourage this. Write down a list of potential words and look at them over a few days. Which word keeps jumping out at you? Which one seems powerful and resonant? This process is much more about 'feeling' than thinking. As a reminder, some resonant words include:

- Care
- Connection
- Grace
- Wholeness
- Home
- Beauty
- Love
- Friendship
- Joy
- Health
- Peace
- Kindness
- Compassion
- Purpose
- Possibility
- Affection

APPENDIX B: YOUR SENTENCE

An ideal sentence either contains or supports the word you have chosen in Appendix A. It should be obvious that the sentence is an extension or explanation of your word. Your sentence should also be very descriptive and simple. Every word should help convey the essence of what you are doing and why it is important or powerful.

My Sentence is*:

*Write your sentence in this space or on a separate piece of paper

Practice speaking your sentence to other people. Ask them to read it as well. Then ask them to tell you what they think you are doing. Are they accurate? Do they get the idea? If they cannot repeat back to you what you are trying to convey then your sentence needs more work.   This sentence is the basis for everything you are about to do. Make it count!

APPENDIX C: YOUR PARAGRAPH

Like your sentence, your paragraph should be very descriptive and powerful. It should contain all the information necessary to get the how, what, who, where and why of what you are proposing to build.

A helpful way to create your paragraph is to break the sentence down into parts, and give each part its own sentence. If your sentence says you are 'creating software', for example, dedicate a sentence to describing the software, what it does, and how it will benefit the user. Each component of your sentence can be expanded upon to make a part of your paragraph. Then make sure your paragraph makes sense: It should have an opening sentence that conveys the idea (maybe it is your sentence from above) and a closing sentence that conveys passion and purpose.

My Paragraph is*:

*Write your paragraph in this space or on a separate piece of paper

Now, just like your sentence, go out and test your paragraph. Do people understand what you mean? Do they have any unanswered questions? Is anything missing? If it does not resonate or create understanding, then re-write the paragraph until it does.

APPENDIX D: YOUR SUMMARY

The summary is an expansion of the paragraph. I like to put my paragraph (developed in Appendix C) first in my summary so that if the reader only went as far as the opening they would at least get an overview of what I was trying to do. This is not necessary, however, as the main point of the opening paragraph is to describe the compelling nature of the idea more than anything else.

For each of the numbers below, one paragraph should suffice, although in some cases you might go to a second. If you find yourself writing more than two paragraphs on any one of these subjects, it is time to condense your thoughts and be more succinct in your writing. The point is to be able to thoroughly describe your business in two pages, not say everything about what you are trying to do.

I recommend you start by simply filling in the blanks. Then you can go back and 'smooth' the paragraphs so that they flow from one to the other nicely.

1. The idea

Describe your idea. If it works, this may be the same paragraph you constructed above (in this space or on a separate piece of paper or document)

2. The market

Describe your market and the key buyers

3. The product

Describe your product or service offering

4. Operations

Describe how you will run your business

5. Technology

Describe any technology you intend to use

6. Marketing and Sales

Describe how you intend to market or sell your product or service

7. Business Model

Describe your major revenue sources and costs

8. Strategy and competitive landscape

Describe your competition and how you fit into the market

9. Financing needs and Corporate Structure

Describe the structure of your company and how much money you will need

10. Bios

Describe the people involved and why they are perfect for this business

Once you have filled in each section, combine all the paragraphs into one document and read the entire thing beginning to end. Does it make sense? Does it flow? Go back and add or remove any content that seems out of place. Smooth the paragraphs so that they flow nicely from one to the other. Read it again. Does your writing tell a compelling story? If it does not, look for what is missing. Is it exciting and interesting? If you had money, would you invest? If you find yourself getting excited as you read, then you are on the right track!

As you might be able to tell, this is not a one-time process. When writing my summaries I will sometimes re-read and edit the document 10 to 15 times! I tend to write too much in my documents at first, so I find myself word-smithing, condensing, and combining sentences. The goal is to get to 2 pages, maybe 2.5 to 3, but no more. It helps to get someone else to read it. Ask them what is exciting, what works, what seems unnecessary. Tighten, edit and re-visit. Put it away for a day or two and then read it fresh again. In this process you will find yourself clarifying your positions and tightening your thinking. This is the point. The document itself is merely a vehicle.

Dive in! You cannot 'fail' at this. You can only learn, grow and improve!

APPENDIX E: YOUR NUMBERS

Creating a spreadsheet is a way to tell your story through numbers. You can show how and when you will make money, and where you will spend that money in support of your ongoing operations. In your summary you will have a paragraph that describes your business model and the assumptions you make. In your spreadsheet you will 'mirror' that description by showing exactly when and how the business model will unfold. In the beginning you will have mainly costs. At some point you will start to bring in revenue. And then your costs may increase as you hire staff and pay for resources to support your operations. This will, in turn, increase your revenue. Growing a profitable enterprise is a series of growth steps that can be reflected in numbers on a time-based spreadsheet.

On the following pages are a series of blank spreadsheet templates. I encourage you to use them as guides. I have found them to be very helpful in creating a simple and compelling plan that is easy to read and manipulate. As you can see, there are revenues and costs down the left-hand side, and time across the top. Your goal is to show when and how you will make or spend money. You can't possibly know everything (especially as time gets further out) but you *can* make educated guesses and do research to make strong assumptions. The point is to *fill in this spreadsheet*, and not leave your numbers up to chance.

Before you get started you will need to do a couple of things:

1. Learn Excel or another spreadsheet program. Excel is the industry standard, but there are certainly other, cheaper, options. Generally, spreadsheets are simply forms that allow you to place formulas in each cell. The formulas can be constructed to automatically add, subtract, multiply, divide, calculate interest, use percentages, and a very, very large number of other functions. If you learn how you use a spreadsheet well, then you will have immediately learned a very important business skill. In the days before spreadsheets it took hours and hours to calculate rows and columns of numbers. And the mistakes were constant. This process has been made incredibly easy with current spreadsheet software. Learn it!

2. Accept that you can't know everything. The spreadsheet is a hypothesis based on your current understanding of the business and industry. You are trying to tell a story about what you *think* will happen, not what you *know* will occur. For this reason you will want to be conservative in your

estimates. Build in 'buffers' to your numbers so that if you are wrong (i.e. too high on the revenues or too low on the costs) you will at least minimize the impact on profit. Do your research, make an estimate, then move on.

3. Be prepared to iterate. I look at spreadsheets more like 'control panels' that I can play with. I set up the spreadsheet, put in some initial numbers, then play around with the assumptions to see what will happen. Change your growth rate or unit sales assumptions, and see what happens. Watch the profit go up and down as you change your numbers. If you have set up your formulas well, then you can change the numbers as much as you want and the spreadsheet will do all the calculating for you.

4. Lay out your assumptions. Assumptions are the numbers that feed the spreadsheet. Your revenues, for example, will be based on how many units you think you can sell per month. How many units you can sell is based on the size of the market and the percentage of the market you think you can get to buy what you are selling. If there are 1,000 people in your market, and you think you can sell to 1% of them in the first year, then you will sell 100 units in the first year. If you assume your price is $500 per unit, then you will make $50,000 in the first year ($500 x 100). These are your assumptions, and they drive the numbers you put in the revenue line on your spreadsheet. It is even better if you can put the assumptions on the spreadsheet and then use them to

calculate the cells in your model. That way if you decide to change an assumption (say price) the spreadsheet will show immediately how your change affects your profit.

OK, so get started by re-creating the following spreadsheets in Excel or another program*. Place formulas into the cells so that each column and row calculates as shown. Then set your assumptions and start putting numbers in the cells. Again, you can't 'fail' at this. You can only learn!

If you cannot read these spreadsheets or would like a free template, please go to kchildreth.com/freedownloads

YEAR 1	Jan	Feb	Mar	Apr	May	Jun	Jul	Aug	Sep	Oct	Nov	Dec	Total
Revenues													
Revenue Stream 1													
Revenue Stream 2													
Revenue Stream 3													
Total Revenue													
Cost of Revenues													
Cost 1													
Cost 2													
Cost 3													
Net Direct Costs													
Net Revenues													
Costs													
Employees													
Employee 1													
Employee 2													
Employee 3													
Employee 4													
Rent													
Utilities													
Supplies Equip													
Legal Fees													
Accounting/Tax													
Professional Fees													
Marketing													
Travel													
Operating Expenses													
Web Development													
Site Management													
Net Costs													
Profit/Loss													

	Q1	Q2	Q3	Q4	Total		Year 3	Year 4	Year 5
Revenues									
Revenue Stream 1									
Revenue Stream 2									
Revenue Stream 3									
Total Revenue									
Cost of Revenues									
Cost 1									
Cost 2									
Cost 3									
Net Direct Costs									
Net Revenues									
Costs									
Employees									
Employee 1									
Employee 2									
Employee 3									
Employee 4									
Rent									
Utilities									
Supplies Equip									
Legal Fees									
Accounting/Tax									
Professional Fees									
Marketing									
Travel									
Operating Expenses									
Web Development									
Site Management									
Net Costs									
Profit/Loss									

(Header: **YEAR 2** spans Q1–Q4 and Total columns)

Hopefully you will have gained something through this process. This step is very important because the numbers are the 'meat' of any business. In my experience the number 1 reason a small business will struggle is due to a lack of attention to these numbers. When you think through your revenues and expenditures, you can both budget and measure your operations. You can anticipate cash needs and see the 'big picture' behind your growth. When you avoid this step you are, essentially, walking into a minefield blindfolded. It is just a matter of time before something unexpected blows up your business.

The spreadsheet is the only part of the plan I encourage my clients to treat as a living document. You should look at it often, compare it to actual, and see if you guessed right. If an investor comes knocking, you will need to know these numbers like the back of your hand. The more competent you are with your spreadsheet, the more likely you are to be successful!

APPENDIX F: RADIANCE HAIR SALON EXAMPLE

In order to provide an example of the business planning process, I have chosen to create a small, local hair salon that is just beginning its start-up process. It is purposefully simple. I wanted to use a business that most people would understand, and be able to provide concrete, relatable numbers. Your content may be far more complex or just as simple, but either way it will follow the same outline and process.

In my 30 plus years in business I have never come across a business that was 'too complex' to plan. I find that anyone claiming that their business can't be planned is, usually, just unwilling to go through the effort. You can structure and estimate just about anything, so don't fool yourself by thinking that this example does not apply to you. I have both written and taught plans that range from simple retail outlets to internet sites to highly complex video monitoring software and equipment providers. All of them were 2-3 pages long and took the exact form shown below.

As you go through your process, refer to this from time to time if you get stuck. It might help you sort through any confusion.

Radiance Hair Salon

The Word: *Beauty*

I choose this word because:

I love to help people feel beautiful. When I cut and style a client's hair I love to see them light up when I am done. They look really happy when they look at themselves, and that makes me feel very good. I feel like I am doing something important in the world.

The Sentence:

I am creating a hair salon where my stylists and I help our clients feel beautiful both inside and out.*

*Notice that this business is more than a simple hair salon. It is actually a place where people can feel beautiful. Which is more 'resonant' to you...a barber shop or a place to feel beautiful? Which contains love?

The Paragraph:

I am creating a hair salon where my stylists and I help our clients feel beautiful both inside and out. I intend to attract customers by making the salon very beautiful both inside and out. I also intend to use the latest equipment and products. My salon will be located in a highly accessible area downtown, have 15 stations, and be staffed by highly trained and very personable stylists. I will need approximately $20,000 to get my project off the ground and intend to be profitable by the end of the first year. I am very excited to be doing this because I *love to help people feel beautiful and good about themselves!**

*In this example I am using "I" as the pronoun, but it can be "we" or even person-neutral. If you are creating a more complex company, such as a software firm or manufacturing concern, you will likely have more detail. I am using a hair salon because it is simple and well known. No matter what type of business, however, the key is to create an overview that discusses all the main points yet leaves the listener wanting more.

The Summary

Radiance Salon

Where Everyone Leaves Beautiful

I am creating a hair salon where my stylists and I help our clients feel beautiful both inside and out. I intend to attract customers by making the salon very beautiful both inside and out. I also intend to use the latest equipment and products. My salon will be located in a highly accessible area downtown, have 15 stations, and be staffed by highly trained and very personable stylists. I will need approximately $20,000 to get my project off the ground and intend to be profitable by the end of the first year. I am very excited to be doing this because I love to help people feel beautiful and good about themselves!

In my town there are 50,000 people, all of whom get a haircut at least 11 times per year. On average, women get a haircut once a month, while men get a haircut every 6-7 weeks. Children typically get a haircut once every 3 months. If I assume that 10% of the population are children under 10 and 50% of the population are women, then there are approximately 537,000 haircuts in our *town each year! If each haircut costs, on average, $50 then the total market size is $26,850,000!*

Our service will be men's, women's and children's haircuts and styling. Men's and children's haircuts are very straightforward. Women's cuts will also include coloring, permanents, extensions and various other offerings. Our offering will be special because we intend to give a free wash and 10 min neck massage with each cut.

Operationally, we will need 10 chairs, mirrors, 2 wash stations, a bathroom, a small kitchen (for hot tea, etc), 3 hair dryers and a receptionist area. Each stylist will bring their own cutting and styling equipment, but we will also have 3 full sets for emergency purposes. We will also have a full range of product on offer from Nexxus and perhaps one or two other vendors. Inventory will be kept as low as possible to minimize storage, but there will be enough to last at least 2 months.

We will have a very simple web site that lists our stylists, our contact information, and our service offerings. In the future we would like to allow customers to schedule appointments via the site, but for now it will all be done over the phone. We will market the salon in four ways: On the internet (yelp, etc), in the local newspaper, with flyers around town, and via business cards in neighboring shops. We also intend to give a 'word of mouth' referral bonus to each existing customer. Our logo and messaging will convey beauty, kindness and warmth. The storefront will be welcoming and our staff very friendly and courteous.

The business model for a hair salon is very well known. There are two main sources of revenue: Hair services and product sales. We will price our hair *services competitively (see the attached price sheet), and use the standard pricing for all products. The costs associated with running the business are high in the beginning due to initial investment, but become consistent as the operations mature. The most significant operational costs will be rent, power and insurance. See the attached spreadsheet for details on the estimated costs. We anticipate generating a profit after about ____ months of operations, and will be seeking to maintain a ____ % profit margin on an ongoing basis. Given our assumptions about traffic and customer volume, we intend to be generating $____ in monthly profit by the second year. If we gain a large customer base then we could be generating over $_____ per year in profit by the 3rd and 4th years.*

In our town there are 10 other hair salons, located within a 10 mile radius. My salon would make 11. Given the size of the market, if split evenly, each salon can make approximately $244,000 per year. We intend to generate more than our share, as shown by our spreadsheet, because we are going to offer a wider range of products and a level of customer care that is far beyond anything anyone in this town has ever seen. Our difference will be our stylists, who will be hired for their people-skills and inherent kindness. We believe that this, along with our quality product, will create a very strong and loyal customer base.

My company will be organized as an LLC in the state of California. I will be the sole owner and initial investor. I will need $20,000 to get this business off the ground. I intend to use $10,000 I have in savings and borrow the rest from my family at 5% interest. Once I get up and running I will apply for a credit line from my local bank to cover the ups and downs of cash flow that are typical of a salon with seasonal customer flows.

I will be the sole owner of this company and am the perfect person to start this *business. I come from a long line of entrepreneurs and so have an entire family from which to draw support and knowledge. I also have over 10 years of hair styling experience and have graduated from one of the nation's top styling schools. I am the perfect person to do this and am excited to start making people beautiful!**

*This is an unusually short example because of the small, local nature of the business and the very well known business model. It is intended as a guide only...yours may be longer or shorter depending on how much information you find about your market and the nature of your products. In any event, remember the write up should never be more than 3 pages.

The Numbers:

Assumptions

- *Clients will be split 40/40/10 men/women/children*
- *Average men's cut will be $25, women's $75, children's $20*
- *Month to month growth in sales in first year will be 15%*
- *Second year quarter to quarter growth will be 20%*
- *Growth will slow to 10% per year in years 3-5*
- *Cost of revenues are 50% (what I pay the stylist)*
- *Direct employees will be 2 (me at $24K per year and an assistant hired in June for $12K per year)*
- *Employee burden will be 25% for health care*
- *Another employee will be added in Year 3 for $24K to help with the volume**

If you cannot read these spreadsheets or would like a free example, please go to

kchildreth.com/freedownload.

YEAR 1

	Price	Jan	Feb	Mar	Apr	May	Jun	Jul	Aug	Sep	Oct	Nov	Dec	Total
Revenues														
Men's Cuts	$25	$1,125	$1,294	$1,488	$1,711	$1,968	$2,263	$2,602	$2,993	$3,441	$3,958	$4,551	$5,234	$32,627
Women's Cuts	$75	$3,375	$3,881	$4,453	$5,133	$5,903	$6,788	$7,807	$8,978	$10,324	$11,873	$13,654	$15,702	$97,881
Children's Cuts	$20	$200	$230	$255	$304	$350	$402	$463	$532	$612	$704	$809	$930	$5,800
Gross Revenue		$4,700	$5,405	$6,216	$7,148	$8,220	$9,453	$10,871	$12,502	$14,377	$16,534	$19,014	$21,866	$136,308
Cost of Revenues	50%	$2,350	$2,703	$3,108	$3,574	$4,110	$4,727	$5,436	$6,251	$7,189	$8,267	$9,507	$10,933	$68,154
Net Revenues		$2,350	$2,703	$3,108	$3,574	$4,110	$4,727	$5,436	$6,251	$7,189	$8,267	$9,507	$10,933	$68,154
Costs														
Employees		$2,500	$2,500	$2,500	$2,500	$2,500	$4,375	$4,375	$4,375	$4,375	$4,375	$4,375	$4,375	$43,125
Rent		$1,000	$1,000	$1,000	$1,000	$1,000	$1,000	$1,000	$1,000	$1,000	$1,000	$1,000	$1,000	$12,000
Utilities		$150	$150	$150	$150	$150	$150	$150	$150	$150	$150	$150	$150	$1,800
Equipment		$10,000	$1,000	$200	$200	$200	$200	$200	$200	$200	$200	$200	$200	$13,000
Legal Fees		$500	$200	$200	$200	$200	$200	$200	$200	$200	$200	$200	$200	$2,700
Accounting/Tax		$200	$200	$200	$200	$200	$200	$200	$200	$200	$200	$200	$200	$2,400
Marketing		$2,000	$1,000	$500	$500	$500	$500	$500	$500	$500	$500	$500	$500	$8,000
Travel		$0	$0	$0	$0	$0	$0	$0	$0	$0	$0	$0	$0	$0
Web Development		$2,000	$500	$0	$0	$0	$0	$0	$0	$0	$0	$0	$0	$2,500
Site Management		$100	$100	$100	$100	$100	$100	$100	$100	$100	$100	$100	$100	$1,200
Net Costs		$18,450	$6,650	$4,850	$4,850	$4,850	$6,725	$6,725	$6,725	$6,725	$6,725	$6,725	$6,725	$86,725
Profit/Loss		($16,100)	($3,948)	($1,742)	($1,276)	($740)	($1,998)	($1,289)	($474)	$464	$1,542	$2,782	$4,208	($18,571)

YEAR 2

	Q1	Q2	Q3	Q4	Total	Year 3	Year 4	Year 5
Revenues								
Men's Cuts	$ 15,702	$ 18,842	$ 22,611	$ 27,133	$ 84,287	$ 92,716	$ 101,988	$ 112,186
Women's Cuts	$ 47,105	$ 56,527	$ 67,832	$ 81,398	$ 252,862	$ 278,148	$ 305,963	$ 336,559
Children's Cuts	$ 2,791	$ 3,350	$ 4,020	$ 4,824	$ 14,984	$ 16,483	$ 18,131	$ 19,944
Gross Revenue	$ 65,599	$ 78,718	$ 94,462	$ 113,355	$ 352,134	$ 387,347	$ 426,082	$ 468,690
Cost of Revenues	$ 32,799	$ 39,359	$ 47,231	$ 56,677	$ 176,067	$ 193,674	$ 213,041	$ 234,345
Net Revenues	$ 32,799	$ 39,359	$ 47,231	$ 56,677	$ 176,067	$ 193,674	$ 213,041	$ 234,345
Costs								
Employees	$ 13,125	$ 13,125	$ 13,125	$ 13,125	$ 52,500	$ 76,500	$ 76,500	$ 76,500
Rent	$ 3,000	$ 3,000	$ 3,000	$ 3,000	$ 12,000	$ 13,200	$ 13,200	$ 13,200
Utilities	$ 450	$ 450	$ 450	$ 450	$ 1,800	$ 1,980	$ 1,980	$ 1,980
Equipment	$ 600	$ 600	$ 600	$ 600	$ 2,400	$ 2,640	$ 2,640	$ 2,640
Legal Fees	$ 600	$ 600	$ 600	$ 600	$ 2,400	$ 2,640	$ 2,640	$ 2,640
Accounting/Tax	$ 600	$ 600	$ 600	$ 600	$ 2,400	$ 2,640	$ 2,640	$ 2,640
Marketing	$ 1,500	$ 1,500	$ 1,500	$ 1,500	$ 6,000	$ 6,600	$ 6,600	$ 6,600
Travel	$ -	$ -	$ -	$ -	$ -	$ -	$ -	$ -
Web Development	$ -	$ -	$ -	$ -	$ -	$ -	$ -	$ -
Site Management	$ 300	$ 300	$ 300	$ 300	$ 1,200	$ 1,320	$ 1,320	$ 1,320
Net Costs	$ 20,175	$ 20,175	$ 20,175	$ 20,175	$ 80,700	$ 107,520	$ 107,520	$ 107,520
Profit/Loss	$ 12,624	$ 19,184	$ 27,056	$ 36,502	$ 95,367	$ 86,154	$ 105,521	$ 126,825

*Looking at these spreadsheets you can see a few things right away. First, the company will operate at a deficit for the first 7 months, which is entirely predictable and natural. Whenever you start something you must assume that you will need capital ($) to get it up and running. The only question is 'how much?' As you can see the total amount needed to cover the deficit is $18,571, which is consistent with the written plan expecting to need $20,000. We recommend putting a 'buffer' on the amount you need in order to make sure you have enough money. Second, you can see that the company becomes profitable in years 2-5. This profit can be then redistributed to the owner. Last, you can see that with a spreadsheet you now have a platform on which to 'play around' with the numbers and see what happens to your profit. Watch how the numbers change when you:

- Increase or decrease your price
- Increase or decrease your sales volume (or growth rates)
- Pay yourself or your employees more
- Rent a bigger space sometime during the year
- Spend more on marketing

If you have created your spreadsheet well each of these factors will change the profits and give you an idea of what you can and cannot do with your money. A well-built spreadsheet is a powerful tool!

ABOUT THE AUTHOR

 K.C. HILDRETH is a successful entrepreneur, coach and business consultant who has founded or co-founded 8 companies, been a strategy and technology consultant to Fortune 50 telecommunications and financial services companies, and worked for the banking department of a major law firm on Wall Street and Capitol Hill. K.C. was one of the founders of a television technology company that sold for $80 million in 2005 and, in his various career incarnations, has occupied roles including board member, CEO, CTO, COO and investor…as well as salesperson, paralegal and stock-clerk.

K.C. holds a BA in Political Science from Ohio Wesleyan University, an MBA from The University of Virginia Darden School of Business, an MS in Information Systems from The University of Virginia McIntire School of Commerce, and an MA in Spiritual Psychology from the University of Santa Monica. K.C. writes, speaks and works with the deep belief that every person on this planet has a powerful gift, and can choose to use that gift to become greater than they ever imagined.

K.C. lives in Manhattan Beach, CA — www.kchildreth.com

www.ingramcontent.com/pod-product-compliance
Lightning Source LLC
Chambersburg PA
CBHW071758170526
45167CB00003B/1080